Angel
CLOUD
POETRY

Angel CLOUD POETRY

THE JASMINE OF THE NIGHT

DAVID P. CARLSON

ARPress
ILLUMINATING IDEAS
EMPOWERING VOICES

Scripture quotations marked KJV are from the Holy Bible, King James Version (Authorization Version). First Published in 1611. Quoted from the KJV Classic Reference Bible, Copyright © 1983 by The Zondervan Corporation.

ARPress
45 Dan Road Suite 36
Canton MA 02021

Hotline: 1(800) 220-7660
Fax: 1(855) 752-6001

Ordering Information:
Quantity sales. Special discounts are available on quantity purchases by corporations, associations, and others. For details, contact the publisher at the address above.

Printed in the United States of America.

ISBN-13:   Paperback   979-8-89356-997-1
           eBook   979-8-89356-998-8
           Harback   979-8-89356-999-5

Library of Congress Control Number: 2024911169

Table of Contents

Acknowledgements

BY DAVID P. CARLSON

Special thanks to Becky Campbell for her consistent support with her many talents that have made these poems artistically legible.

Also, of course, to my wife, Linda, many thanks for her patience and daily encouragements. Without her devotion, love, and faith the inspiration for each poem would have never been manifested on paper.

Finally without my salvation, (provided by the Ancient of Days, God the Father of all the ages, Creator of all that has ever existed) and without the ultimate sacrifice of His only begotten son, Jesus of Nazareth for the sins of all mankind all combined, His mercy, sacrifice and love (these His three essential elements) I would have no reason or compulsion to express any passion worth pursuing— "all would be vanity".

Life Between the Lines

BY DAVID P. CARLSON

Poetry, a series of written events all conspiring to force the reader to recall a multitude of people, places and things so remote (yet so greatly inhabited by the beauty of so many painful events) that they so unwillingly paint a portrait of themselves so vivid that reality yields to the divine awareness of a conscious serenity, so complex that all (so simply put) are sadly mundane; Unforeseen and suddenly this solitary life burst upon the scene, confronts the risings in his mind, then kneels to the descending light of time and grace, affirms the course, then steps across the line so quickly drawn; With a stuttering gasp and a chocking hiss, he speaks the words, "Amen, so be it, so now it is." Now truth has been revived as it comes to light in one dark corner of his mind: there beneath the shadowed veil now reveals a man couched and pale, clad in a coat of mail; content to shun the light of the poet's pen. So now he stands, now to embrace the waiting hope for a life well spent, all within the realm of the poet's spin on a life within, never to be content to die again, all propelled by the tip of the poet's pen—This book was written for one purpose and one purpose only, which is for you to view your life behind, yet through this thin veneer of words and phrases, stories and allegories, all created to blend from within (you the reader) personal considerations of specific recollections of times, (ill or well spent) – but now content to attempt to climb above your future's considerable mountains of compilations.

These poems (as is life itself) without a purpose or a point are as trees without limbs or leaves, no trunk or bark, no roots or seeds to grow, could never become a shade for that next generation—please attempt to read, then bask in some related truth—Take a mental sabbatical and say, "That's what I'll do for the rest of my days"—and so is the fruit of enlightenment of so many trees of truth—all within your reach upon heaven's special ladders—each rung a book, each step a gate that swings forever wider, so as to view the world around and your place in life, three-score and six rungs higher.

The Miracle of Transformation

BY DAVID P. CARLSON

In 1953 the Spirit of God drew me out of the pew and into the aisle and down to accept my Lord's salvation. I don't remember what Brother (Rev. Lunsford) said, but I'll never forget the joy of that nine year old boy.

—Nineteen years later—

I often wonder what Brother (Rev. C.C. Hurst) thought that night when the doorbell rang—probably, "who can that be at this time of night," or "what major problem am I about to face this time?" Hesitantly he opened the door and I heard him say, "Can I help you?" and then, "Oh, David, what's the problem?" I had been at his church before (he immediately recognized sister Bozman's granddaughter's bar-room boyfriend—Me!!) Well, there we were; myself, my girlfriend, and my best friend, J.B White, standing there on the porch. We had been arguing about if God was real over a couple of six-packs (or more maybe). I'm sure he could smell the beer on my breath, but believe it or not, he said, "Let's go over to the church and talk this over. It wasn't long that he cut to the chase and said, "David, do you want to give your life back to the Lord tonight and receive him as Lord and Savior?" I said, "Yes, Pastor Hurst, I do." I was immediately completely sober. He then led me in the sinner's prayer and that was that. My friend J.B. was stunned, to say the least, and, not doubt, highly disappointed in me. Brother Hurst asked J.B., "How about you son?" J.B. stormed out with an unlit cigarette dangling from his mouth; I think I even heard him curse a little. We had been friends for at least ten years, but everything changed that night. We never really ever spoke again to each other up to the time he died about 15 years later.

Well, I began to display, at that point, a major change. Church was my life and God began to mold me into a new man. I married my girlfriend, (sister Bozman's granddaughter) who had 3 children from former marriages already. Before we married in God's presence, one night he spoke to me to the effect, "I've given you a new life, now will you have a problem with raising 3 children as your own?" I said, "Yes, Lord, I will do it."

Well, things got better and better. We bought a small trailer (my parents were a bit skeptical about me taking on such a responsibility). But finally they cane around and supported my decision since they were so thrilled that I had changed from a bar-room brawler to a Bible-toting Christian. They were totally convinced something wonderful had happened and said "Amen!"

—But the best was yet to come!!!—

One night I took JoAnn and Mary (ages 3 and 6) to a church revival. That night I told Brother Hurst, "I know I'm saved and things are going great, but something is missing. He prayed for me. After the service we headed home. On the way, it seemed the Lord brought to my remembrance an incident that had happened years before my God-drawn

Conversion. We had been partying, drinking, drugging, etc, on a little beach in a Bayside, TX. I had a little boat that me and J.B. had built (a red, all wood, flat-bottom boat). It wasn't real big but it was heavy. At one point I ended up on that boat by myself. Everybody else was up on the shore. I kind of panicked when I realized it was almost dark and I was pretty high and I was drifting out into the bay. Everybody thought that was pretty funny, but it wasn't. I could have ended up all night drifting to who knows where. When that dawned on me, I grabbed the anchor and threw it in—guess what? It wasn't tied on to the boat's rope!! I only had one option—I grabbed the rope and jumped in the water that came just below my chest. I began the long, arduous task of pulling that boat back to the shore which took about what seemed hours. But finally I made it to the shore. Everybody got a big laugh out of that. As I was thinking about that experience going up on the 13th block of N. Ave. D that night, it was like God said, "that boat was all those sins I have forgiven you for"—then I saw God cut the rope!! I was free from that great enormous weight, and friend, I went nuts!!! It was a rush had never experienced! I took the girls home and told my wife what had happened and that I had to find brother Hurst and let him know too. I went by my parent's house and literally burst in and told them that something wonderful had happened!! I think they thought I was on drugs, drunk or just gone crazy again. Next morning I was still filled with that wonderful anointing that has never, to this day, subsided. Well, forty-two years have come and gone and I've been blessed with 3 children of my own. I've been through many trials including my wife's death in 1996 of leukemia.

Then in 1998 God blessed me with Linda, and life has never been better!! Old things passed away forty-two years ago, and all things just keep getting newer!!!

Winter's Hand

I stand in winter's robe, clutching warmth where I can.
I reach to feel the cold night wind
Tears on winters face I touch
Her sadness holds me, clutching warmth where she can.
I take her hand, I understand
Her tears splash, then turn to ice
A winters night has found a friend.

—David Paul Carlson

As Published by
The National Library of Peotry

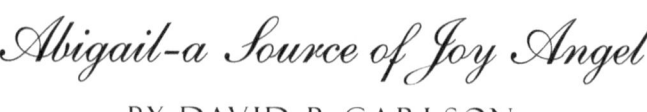

Abigail-a Source of Joy Angel

BY DAVID P. CARLSON

Sweetly silent this tender life has slipped away, passing peacefully along her days as a springtime song of praise to the Lord of the great beyond. This soul-full child, a melody as pure as a gentle wind upon this place of her eternal rest, now left to sway upon countless waves of heaven's symphonic melodies, her spirit strolls through care-free days with her friends, the angels, there to guide her on all her ways. As this resplendent angelic child resides there within her songs she hums a peasant tune for Mom and Dad to hear there within their dreams. With a perfect pirouette she spins, then turns again to skip along to find a place to count the days when her life will once again meet those cherished ones, her family and those future friends on that bright and sun-bathed day, where they all together can sing as one in perfect harmony the song of the redeemed.

Angel Cloud

BY DAVID P. CARLSON

Misty vapors merge, then mingle as a trailing wisp from her
rainbow-laced wedding grown; angel cloud then serenely drifts
across in stark contrast to the blues and greens and garnished
golds of the sunlit knolls of yesterday, today and forever.
Her presence tolls, enunciating a place in the time where poetic lines
will be inscribed upon a mind to reflect the vision there for countless
souls, there to be enthralled at the sight of this heavenly radiance
of her multi-colored glow; a divine reflection from the promised
one who set the bow there in creation's days of old, who proclaimed
the hopes and dreams of yesterday, today and forever. As he swirled
the clouds, he donned his hand with a satin brush to slash the sky
with a grand array of illuminated prism shades galore, to forge the
supreme depiction of the angle cloud in all her splendid glory. Now
I say, "she was a sight to behold in her classic, wind-drawn surrey."

Angel in the Cloud—to God Be the Glory Is She Relevant?

BY DAVID P. CARLSON

She is relevant because each poem mirrors society, from coal miners to the Boston bombing, from wars abroad to your battles deep within, from the finger of God to the pointed sword at the devil's head. With all that this book is, it screams "It's not in theory, it's all relevant!!"

Many Books, in some ways, mimic others. This book when it was finished (even though I wrote it), made me wonder from whom it was I stole it. But then I recognized the true Author is truly like no other—the Holy Spirit, rightly noted, penned each word because to God I give the glory, and God has deemed that relevant to the angel in the cloud for me to meet the angels of Revelation.

A Penthouse View of the Last Days

BY DAVID P. CARLSON

Since all the encroachments of escalating darkness throughout all
the descending centuries since time began, these Last Days still
contain, though diminished, a strain of hope I call the isthmus lane
which runs between Veracity's efficiency apartments and the perfidy
acute-occult townhouse dwellings along the esplanade of Satanic
Avenue and Demonic Drive; this scenic route along the shore is better
known to those that dwell therein as the only way to drive through
the storms of Christendom to avoid the chance that they might join.
Now the byways have been paved by the terroristic tar of barbarism,
trafficking winds around the curbs and lines of the interstate of human
souls. All life has been exploited—biblical principles—prophecies
and all those holy covenants are the only lanes still left to connect
this Christian isthmus to the stars—our home and God alone.

This final esplanade along the shore of eternity has turned out to be
nothing more than the earth's back door, and anathema where fools
may dwell, void of wit or clearness. So here, there within their final
domain these nimble-fingered identity thieves jeer, then flaunt their
ill-gotten gains, having done all they can to authenticate their claim
to fame as their name proclaimers, "The defiant ones". So now, as
their days wind up and down they slow their pace, and as time expires
they settle down in their pre-assigned resting place, there to hang
their hats at the tavern's inn, better known in this world below as
the leper's den, --a cozy little colony growing up in leaps and bounds
with an equally nauseating chorus of groans and frantic sounds.

Limp and twisted so describes their minds, bent so as to embrace the
philosophy of Epicurus who believed that pleasure is the chief and
utmost aim in life to gain, but unbeknownst to him another wise man
said, "put a knife to the throat if a man be given to appetite," which
reminds me of another tasteless and hopefully the last production of
gloom and doom, a box-office hit and its final run at a world premiere.

So—here to proudly introduce this classic play, "The Old Grim
Reaper", to describe every scene of a total eclipse of eternal life,
day by day. "I, the Grim Reaper say, yes, I will, and how glad I
am to introduce this darling cast, all draped in various forms of
mass destruction; now how about a hand for the devil's crowd and
their daunting last brigade." What a spectacular and memorable,
but sad conclusion of a world whose hopes and dreams all hinge,
and ultimately depend on Medicaid and Diary Queen.
Now as the world returns as it was before the shout, "Let there be
light!" you hear the cry of the multitudes all slated to return again
to the dark corners of the universe. Total extermination, total
evacuation from this blackened crust we call our molten earth,
that's all that's left to entertain the world's profane, insane, inane,
those bound in chains, all huddled in this bloody field of carnage
where hopes and dreams have been reduced to ash and white-hot
dust, (a final epigram without the wit), there to ponder in the soot
and sludge of the bottomless pit—this finial esplanade you can
avoid by a simple choice—so stay at home and serve the Lord—
enjoy your view from your penthouse suite atop a higher calling.

A Temple's Steeple—
Just a Point In View

BY DAVID P. CARLSON

Temple's steeples spike the sky from coast to coast extending high
above, through those glowing redwood cinders, dancing upwards
from those Sequoia martyrs, back wood mesquite, men of morals,
joining in are those piney woods of contemporary forests, steeped
in Christendom's Ridge, but commentaried versions of Christian
universities, all ascending from the land below, all set ablaze by
a volcano of civilian's civil and mental anthropoidic unrest and
resentfulness, to then again be conjured up at a later date in
some backstreet amphitheater to crank and bend those steeples
down, to slash and chop those postulate points that permeate,
then penetrate their scale-like skin: now resistance to them has
always been excelled by Godly men with didactic tack with such
a verbal thrust it unlooses the fetters from the hearts of men
and women, boys and girls who claim "in god they trust".

The enemy's ultimate task is this, to amend those truths within those
sermonettes of so-called exhortations by men on high (those gray-
bearded ones, schooled by celebrities and their countless groupie
friends of anthropology) that probe their lies into the heavens with
another set of pernicious temple's steeples of pines and needles.

Now the gist of all of this needs not to be revised, transposed, contrived or compromised, so then be deemed a perverted form of veracity (heresies! So charged in some religious forums of duplicity), but truly this well-documented dominant creed does demand the cross on top should be displayed and plainly seen as an eternal and God-penned theme, for without the cross there would be no point to guide the way, nor challenge for us to tread across that swirling and swollen Jordan River of pride to the banks of Eternal Love, there atop those steeple's peaks there upon the other side, a point well-taken to the Cross where there the tip was stained in red by the blood He shed to emphasize our so-called common and mundane steeples pointing to the skies.

Beyond the Generational Gap

BY DAVID P. CARLSON

This generation chants peace on earth with paradigmal slants,
leaning on with each inflection toward the garbed cry of suicidal
insurrection—although vague, more or less, still they will describe
what they strive to represent as the path to attain the plan for legal
social status. Political winds unfurl their flags to the dismay of many
bewildered citizens. What is this flag they dare to fly above this
nation's hallowed ground—nothing more than a counterfeit of what
was once held dear—how paradigmatic, totally driven by another
culture's instincts to be furiously ambiguous, yet they still retain the
name "a paradigm of shame or blame" however your inflections are
applied, --a literary algorithm sifting through this plethora of symbolic
words to describe their despicable acts, to enhance a so-called paragon
of the piano-man brought to the highest strato-sphereal plain—there
to grapple for all to see the lowest of all degrees, the mesopause,
ninety kilometers above mesosphere, any more would exceed the
boundaries of endless peace in those outer limits of supersonic fears.
Those past generations that once chanted for affinity with God,
now seem faded under continuous conjecture of liberal confederates,
but alas, the trumpet sounds, fading faith rebounds to disgorge
the prose, to retain the rhyme of poetic chimes as the congregation
of the resplendent redeemed rise beyond the boundaries of the
mesopausic ridge, to escape the chants of dying men, driven by
the paradigm of their own dissentions from grace and glory, all
conjoined with no further purpose than to receive for lack of
compassion—thirty-nine lashes on a continual daily basis.

Biblical Poetry (Glory)

ARRANGED BY DAVID P. CARLSON
(KING JAMES VERSION)

Lev. 9:6, 11, 23, 24

V6 and Moses said, This is the thing which the LORD commanded that ye should do: and the glory of the LORD shall appear upto you. V11 And the flesh and the hide he burnt with fire without the camp. V23 And Moses and Aaron went into the tabernacle of the congregation, and came out, and blessed the people: and the glory of the LORD appeared unto all the people. V24 And there came a fire out from before the LORD, and consumed upon the altar the burnt offering and the fat: which when all the people saw, they shouted, and fell on their faces.

I Kings 9:8-9

And at this house, which is high, every one that passeth by it shall be astonished, and shall hiss; and they shall say, Why hath the LORD done thus unto this land, and to this house? V9 And they shall answer, Because they forsook the LORD their God, who brought forth their fathers out of the land of Egypt, and have taken hold upon other gods, and have worshipped them, and served them: therefore hath the LORD brought upon them all this evil.

John 12:46

I am come a light into the world, that whosoever believeth on me should not abide in darkness.

Branches

BY DAVID P. CARLSON

Green and thin now equates to trembling lusts of chlorophylling gel within the veins of leaves from their long extended stems and branches. The relentless gusts of winter's breath bends then twists till all seems lost, all is tossed from side to side till the wind collides, buckles and then subsides again. Motionless, the limbs silently weep and groan, as the tear-like sap flows from those countless leaves and splintered twigs they once caressed (but now sadly and bereaved) as their seed-rich stems, all now strewn by God, there to be whisked away by another late December breeze.

Brine Foam Upon the Shore

BY DAVID P. CARLSON

Through oceans of time and space it seems I catch a glimpse of your
worried face peering out from behind your chin on knees across the
waves of a rising tide to the distant shores of yesterday; As a salty
gust of wind and mist shower you with (as you might pessimistically
describe) minute rocks called sand, I see you hesitate, then step into
the waves. Cold is the foaming brine—some would count each wave
as years, some would say they depict your fallen tears, but I will say,
"Life up your eyes a little higher to view the source of
waves and that ocean of your endless unborn days."
My prayer for you, my dear, is that you will return back to the
shore and once again confess him as your Lord of Lords, and in
that moment you'll see he'll come and leave his love and peace like
brine foam upon your youthful shore for you and yours; never to
recede, always present as the vast and endless sea of eternity.

Divine Design

BY DAVID P. CARLSON

Though thoughts compressed in riddles, then guided through a maze of endless walls of literary vines and flowers, all draped in the premise that all men search for their own divine design: who you are is summarized by what you find concealed between the lines of life's poetic rhyme that connects directly with you alone. As positive depends upon the negative, so the mind and soul finally find resolve to embrace the theme of a continual falling, then rising and overcoming of all of life's onslaughts of disappointments by injecting God's Word and promises into the wound until you see at last the miracle of his divine design spread abroad through you to future generations.

Dream Busters

BY DAVID P. CARLSON

Like a blank piece of paper is this man and his mind, once filled
with the hope he would eventually find that long sought treasure he
buried so well and so deep in the sands of the past where the winds
have since scattered all signs of the path he might have so carelessly
left in the wake of his wrath. Now compelled by only his memories,
he tells how he staked his claim in the dirt, he then so cunningly
lined with his life's perfect work (so he affirms) so worthily priceless
he vigorously boasts is the ultimate cost of all his so well-deserved
trophies, accomplished honors and goals: his claim was his fame you
can instantly tell by his half-hearted smirk he thought he had hidden
so well: surprisingly to me, there in the trash, he furiously retrieved
that old crumpled up map of his lost mine to again be revived by
the sight of that mountain he would again be tempted to climb: now
there in the mine with his arms and hands set in an akimbo-type of
recline (his symbol of pride) he gathers his gold and jewels untold
to be groomed as the grandest prize of all times for all to behold;
his sparkling diamonds all priced at great worth of which, soon he
thinks, all will be viewed by the great men of this earth! But sorely
and painfully obvious were those stones set in rows, elegantly laid
in perfect array, so starkly unnatural the question from within them
begins to unfold—could this be that blank piece of paper, this shell of
a man to be lead so astray that a handful of rocks could be the worth
of the lot of his deed that he has so unfortunately already paid?

Now all is not lost for our misguided friend, for the
price of this lesson could be less than a yen.
Now with one slight adjustment (as a chiropractor may say)
let's dull the peak of his grief by applying my suggested
suggestion with a new set of treasures to seek.
Let go of your map, give up your gold, turn to
the source of all treasures untold—
Return to the Lord—through those tunnels you'll find; deep within
those recesses of forgiveness where therein lies that rich sense of peace
where there he'll fulfill all your needs plus his blessings caressing all
your life's most cherished collections of life-giving seeds. All that is
required is then to simply say, "Lord, I believe, show me the way."

Elliptic Rose

BY DAVID P. CARLSON

Alone the rose sways and bobs in perfect time with her friend the
sympathetic wind, there to be enjoined with their affirimities;
he's there to help caress her sadness she must feel to be the elliptic
rose, alone and tethered to her leafless stem high above the ground
without her leaf embroidered shroud; she knows the wind would
help her if he could, but without her leaves she has no beauty
to behold: now a rose by any other name is still not as sweet as
the leaves that hold her natural lusters bound, that come alive to
entice the petals, to join together, then blossom forth to release the
scent that defines her special fragrance, an essence to be enjoyed
there far above the leaves and far-reaching, bending stems.
Snip, snap, the enemy of her soul separates, eclipsing her leaves of
youthfulness, the memories of the days when she was just a bud upon
the stem of so many yesterdays! Elliptic rose sheared and pruned of
all her dignity, placed within an artificial vase, all set in lines and
rows. In her natural state, her insectic world denies her of her leaves
of green, now bronzed, now brown and speckled on the ground—
these leaves have eyes for there to gaze up tragically to behold those
wilted petals fluttering to the land below. But yet in truth her true
bud has yet to bloom, in death the elliptic rose with one last breath
has strength to gasp, then with one raspy whisper say, "This, of all
my days and now to this one I do succumb, I do concede my life to
cease, in all of this, I still do truly miss all my cherished leaves."

Evil Paladin
"The Grand Scammer"

BY DAVID P. CARLSON

His duplicity emerges from a quiet and meek slightly humble
and apparently compliant frame of a man to arise abruptly as a
cumulonimbus cancerous mass in the northern skies, darkened
by a charging hoard of swirling emotions just beyond the
curvature of his own horizons. This matter obtuse deceiver
consoles the trodden-down only to tangle up their moments
of despair and desperation with perilously, profane verbal
connotation of all their hopes and anxious expectations.
Their spirits were captivated by his grand disguise of perfidiousness
and contorted versions of perverseness, slightly bent and sculptured
by his holy, pious arrogance, perceived to be the enigma prince of
tall, dark, and mysterious, master romancer of the "holly in the
woods" lying, dying novel steeped in science-fiction data, marinated
in a poetic soup of ludus love, with his own sadistic connotations.
From his chair, their director beacons them to review the script,
dress the part, then sip from the golden cup. His deadly dredge,
so to become the ones, the enigma man's queens of solitude
in the infamous darked back stage forest of that immortal
world, all draped in the endless pain of death and sorrow.
Their parts in this Romeo, Jonah, and Juliet tragedy they so
desperately desired to play now welcomes them to their rewards at
center-stage, to then to their surprise-just one solitary line to say

"I relent to not one prayer to pray". (Scratch romances) –the part demands a sacrifice of only common sense- when only now when the play concludes can they comprehend the enigma man's final and remarkably simple scam, even a child can understand his demand to purge the words of truth and love through a maze of mirrored glass to then appear absurd to those desperate hoards of rare but faithful congregated protagonistic wanna-be's, there to emerge atop life's horizons, there to confront the chair where the director of this disaster sits to welcome home his begotten cast for one last curtain-call before the next final and far less alacritous eternal intermission— Now forgive me for this tragic end—so let me recommend salvation's alternative, a well-plotted plan where Jesus Christ will preside as your new director and CEO, where all your future hopes and dreams may flow, to stroll across that emberal stage to receive your golden crown, where never ever is that curtain allowed to come crashing down, or to be drawn to mute that wild applause of countless fulgent throngs of welcoming apologistic angels around the sides of God's golden throne, all there for your eternal and forever certain curtain-call from God, "Hey, come on in, make yourself at home!"

Final Destination

BY DAVID P. CARLSON

Destination, a box car noun, towed sinuously by two or three engine
verbs up Mt. Decision, there to abjectly and conjecturally steam up
to the summit of a place where dreams solidify, then settle down to
suffer. Your destination sometimes lags behind as your conscious mind
winds around the endless tracks of current events which lead in all
directions. This noun called destination, though not designated is oh
so personality enunciated—as youth bends down to take ahold those
verbs emerge, then scamper through the forest, make fly the twigs
and leaves, the trees and shrubs have left behind—some destinations
are but a blur that one observes from afar or maybe from a car that
plunges down, then overturns through the curves and bends, through
the guarding rails of twisted tin to one more monumental crash
before your face meets that wonderful safety device called air in bags
along with its shrapnel and splintered glass; you're blown away into a
comatose-like state, never again to recall the dates of births of any of
your closest kin—so is the end of so many unfortunate few that find
this scenario to be true and destined to be their final destination;
Life is so much better when your destination resonates precisely as a
welcome homing beacon, luming in the distant hills, pulsating with a
resplendent glow, always clear, never perfidious as the obscure, obtuse
chorus of semantical riddles, riddled with vain objectives that never
truly lead to a fruitful God-honored destination. A goal is more than
civil rest or even more than just a test to pass. The road to any worthy
destination has at least a few complications wrapped in butcher paper,
no brilliant bow to be set aside, you only know that where your name
resides it will be written clear within your sight, there upon the map
that leads to that place you hope to soon arrive, there in God's new
Creation on the other side, there to settle in to enjoy the view of the
past at last, from your newly found, eternal, and final destination.

Flight Ninety-Three

BY DAVID P. CARLSON

Her temples quiver, tremble, then sway from side to side like towering steeples in the wake of tornatic winds swirling in the black foreboding skies, all minimized by the stark approaching terror there visualized before her eyes of fleeting, evaporating memories of her closest kin and her own life so soon to end. Her contemplations rise, then fall, pierce through the morning rays to unveil a day of such voraciously correlated streams of representativeness, such a barrage of her reciprocating arteriolar aorta vibrations, so intense as to enhance the river of gushing emotions, all so furiously frightening it grips the heart to imagine the escalating horror that her reeling and bewildered mind and soul must have been forced to feel and see, trapped inside that fuselage of flight Ninety-three—all her plans of yesterday are now neatly stitched upon the fabric of those tear-laced cirrocumulus clouds outside her double-paned window sill, all embroidered by her tormented mind there within the shambles of her resonating family's memories, and as of yet, all forlorn, all too soon to be forgotten: -- then reaching in with heart in hand, she penned her heart-felt letter to those loved ones so soon to be left behind, all viewed and synchronized through her little window in the sky. Some say, where was God on the tragic day? So let me attempt to comfort your endless grief with one resplendent ray of hope— God was there to calm her soul with a peaceful and loving hand to hold on that day of sacrifice for God and country and this nation's soul, all set and parenthesized by what that man said, "Let's rock, let's roll"—a phrase so plain, but yet so bold.

Is this the end? I think not; for all those souls lost that day and all those families' sadness, compounded by countless wrongs untold, the bar was raised for this nation's goal to conceive a plan to cleanse the land of marauding hordes of ruthless men like Osama-bin-Laden. These senseless and brutal acts of war will remind us all for evermore that no matter how high the steeples tower to the sky, or how shrill the engines roar their terror through our skies, none can ne'er compare the gratitude we feel for those brave plenipotentiary souls that took that beleaguered flight (Flight Ninety-three) down to the land below, to that peaceful holy plot of ground of serenely rolling meadows there on the Pennsylvania countryside, instead of downtown in our nation's capitol to be laid to rest alongside our nation's pride and our most-of-all most treasured phrase, "In God we trust".

Fool and the Storm

BY DAVID P. CARLSON

Birds chatter in torrent weather?
What could it mean except fear or ignorance?
Does not the wind or driving rain of flashing lights or bolts
of thunder, curl their feathers, wrench their bodies with
thoughts of a violent end to their seemingly useless lives?
Or is it merely a scene, seen through darting eyes, watching
closely seeing nothing? So it is with some men I know.

Free

BY DAVID P. CARLSON

There is a man in prison in this world today—
There are no locks on the doors but in his mind he's still a
slave. He may escape someday, he may even block the past.
He may walk in the sun and say at last I'm free.

Galactic Time Blood Moon's Risings

BY DAVID P. CARLSON

Rumbling thunder in the night, how courageous are those gathering clouds in early morning's light, there to cause a schism in the atmosphere; such is the swirling of God's celestial mass, so precise as if to point the way to that special day when light denied becomes the shroud across the blood moon's prophetic anno-domini face, there to be our constant meridian reminder of God's ephemeral moment there within translucent space when all of God's collected planets will align with their trailing stones of fire to be as stepping stones for God's elect to skip across as one to that blood moon's peneplain and there to see the Sea of Tranquility transformed from crimson red to virgin green, and then, there we be donned in robes of sky-like blues, bathed in that golden glow of interspace for God's royal introduction, to then behold the face of that ancient architect of all creation, his outer space of garden nebulas, clustered about as glowing clouds of dust and gases, all spread across that massive blue and black star-speckled canvas, so well foretold from fifteen-million light years away in that distant constellations.

Now as the story goes in that splendiferous southern pinwheel galaxy roams that old mythological three-headed serpent known as Hydra, huge, but lack of light, barely seen from afar, (understandably so, being armed with only seventeen less astronomical protagonistic soldier stars). So now in acronical manner, an acronically occurring event, transcending at the moment of life and death, from night to light, in panoramic retrospect looms Crux, also known as the Southern Cross, smaller but among the brightest in the southern hemisphere, only four stars strong! Also there, nestled snuggly beneath the Coal Sack Nebula is that brilliant jewel-box cluster; herein lies God's celestial message, sealed within the heavens, that dominant southern crux of that resplendent cosmic cross now lies embedded as a Biblical heel upon the head of Hydra, herein for all to see that two thousand years ago that star struck three-headed snake, of all astronomical treacheries has received his final blow to reduce his reign as prince of the air to nothing more than another super nova remnant of yesterday, now held in God's utmost distain. Such a grand array of distant stars within the cosmic dust, then displayed just for us there on high to warn the world of an impending end of galactic time. Now another end-time sign a little closer home, so now look up and watch the sky and know "your redemption draweth nigh", signified by another blood moon rising.

God's Way

BY DAVID P. CARLSON

Well, now it's God's way that we know that what we understand to be our Holy Bible, that's of spirit, not of man; Lord and it's God's Way that we be taught, the power of his word, and it's God's way that we live every day what we've learned. Lord, and it's God's way that we be spread like the flowers in the field on the green grass of Jesus beneath the blue skies of God's will. Lord, then it's God's Way that we grow up like the redwoods in the land, there by the brook of Jesus to stand all acts of man. Lord, and it's God's Way that our branches reach out for human souls and gather for the Master a bouquet of red, blue and gold—golden souls. Lord, and it's God's Way that we come through Jesus to the throne and praise God for God's Way, 'cause…..God's Way is the way home. You know sometimes it's God's Way that we feel all alone, but you know that's just God's Way of craving faith, in our sometimes' hearts of stone. And you know, sometimes it's God's Way that fear is something we really feel, but you know, that's just God's Way of tempering strength into out faith and then through us, God can heal. Just remember back through God's Way and that step you just couldn't take alone, and remember it was God's Way that gave you that faith and the strength and courage to go on. Oh, if we could just live everyday God's Way, everyday would be a stepping stone, and everyday we'd be a little stronger, and everyday we'd be just a little closer home.

Gone in Time

BY DAVID P. CARLSON

There I saw a painted sky—two lives stayed to see it.
The lights we saw were gone in time, but to us we had their image.
We touched and weaved the meaning, then saw and felt their leaving,
I tried to stop, hold back the times, but forever
time was gone, even before the ending.

Guy Fawke's Protégé

The Diatribe Rapscallion Lion (the Anti-Christ)

BY DAVID P. CARLSON

(guy n 1; MAN 1a; FELLOW 2: PERSON. Word history—Now.
5 is a holiday in England, and people celebrate it by setting off
fireworks and lighting bonfires. Human likenesses made of tattered
clothes stuffed with hay or rags are burned on the bonfires. The
holiday is called Guy Fawkes Day for a 17th century man who
played a leading role in a plot to blow up the British Parliament
buildings. Fawkes managed to hide 20 barrels of gunpowder in the
cellars of the buildings. However, the plot was discovered before
Fawkes could carry out his plans. He was seized and later put to
death. The human likenesses burned to celebrate the failure of
Guy. Fawkes' plot came to be called guys. The use of the word
was extended to similar figures and then to a person of strange
appearance or dress. In the U.S. the word came to mean simply
"man" or "fellow" and in time came to be used for a person of
either sex [named for Guy Fawkes 1570-1606 English criminal].
(From Webster's Intermediate Dictionary ©
1986 by Merriam Webster, Inc.)

As a lion's roar perks up the vigilant shepherd's ears, the sheep are
scattered, sent scampering through the fields of dark intimidating
hills and shadows. Diatribe well describes this lion's constant arising
pernicious tone in every sentence (derived, then contrived by this
bureaucratic rapscallion type of Guy, a Guy Fawkes plotting wanna-be)
for maximum collateral damage to the common man and to all that
hear his rambling, beaconing and hecklings, all coinciding with
his vile display of mesmerizing the local yokels at their annual

Christmas plays and parties: well, it seems this is the key to all human conversations since time arrived in the back lands of those long-forgotten blacked holes of endless space where there still is stored galaxies of abundant grace for times as these, end of time, end of days. His strategy is that victory goes to the most vociferous orator, thus unlocks the door (as we all know, only one may enter in), but then, when to his chagrin he miserably fails to achieve his goal to trample the source of such lethal confrontations, he slithers back into his hole to plan another bold and sinister plot to overthrow those innocent lambs, so lost and so cold; so now with many final exacting demands this kingly schlemiel swells with pride to think his foe would shrink and fold, then cower down to listen with bated breath his diatribe-able exhortations, so soon he thinks to be recorded by this next generation with admiring poetic flair, garnished with a rare but colorful facsimile of the words he's spoken there: so beneficial they say, so stimulating it extracts the senses so that when confronted by so many confirming attacking facts his eidetic memory decides to forget what he's talking about. Between his lips and brain lie a vast expanse so designed for calculating his next response to the world around (draped in chaos and devastation) to spew out mostly useless information for his robot congregation with their cannibalistic tendencies and unprecedented lack of patience and consistencies. Obviously his diatribe-able personal resemblance of communication has broken off the key within the lock to dash the hopes of men that dare to span the gap, and once again communicate man to man, but this man has defiled himself by his futile attempt to confront she Shepherd of the flock with nothing more than his verbal, inimical arrogance along with his diabolical machination that in turn his beloved dubious gains gain only an angry stare of intense despite from the one and only God of this his cosmic plane and universe. Now with one stroke of divine rebuke he's stricken mute, left with only one sense to hear the words spoken from before the throne, "You have been judged and found wanting!", the last salutation from the master of the one-sided conversation.

King Gull

BY DAVID P. CARLSON

Two circles, islands unmanned, with his feathers picked and
cleaned, his glassy black eyes then dart with instinct's protecting
culture…or maybe with emotions, or is it devotion—maybe human
feelings flow and fly with King Gull. Who knows, not I?
King Gull searches among his subjects—reflect his obligations and
dominates his objectives—King Gull has earned his position and
his subjects obey his decisions—with chest bared, feathers back,
he struts among the citizens—KING GULL UNDISPUTED!!
The sea, the blue-white sky, the breeze that ruffles feather, ALL
KING GULL SENSES. With his kingdom unmolested, he must
feel rewarded, his duties stand fulfilled. Serenity's peace brings
thought of his lofty world, gliding with nature, his natural gift, lands
below his resting place, the sky above his frolicking playground.
HIS KINGDOM STANDS UNMOLESTED
A humming omen, a far-off fear no human yet foreseen—distance
has no meaning, the speed of sound is but a reeling hum King Gull
knows as fear—then the distant fear coils out, strikes King Gull's
ears—unknowing he faces a bird gigantic, a crisis he never knew
sweeps into King Gull's vision. Then silent is his kingdom and
defenseless is his fear—He sees the faces of fear upon his subjects.
He knows his actions are within the eyes of every member. With silent
courage he reflects his kingly state, then collects his instinct's gifts and
call's his leaders forth—He speaks, "Take all and hide beneath the
brush, home is in the path of death. Here we stay, I will tell you when
to go". (Three days pass and King Gull waits). From within the brush,
he fears the sky as death—His subjects wait his decisions (to the mass
he speaks). In our worlds of air you've seen an awesome creature—
across the bay our duties lay unattended—our fear must be forsaken
for across the bay is our home, our beginning, our end, and if our end
must come while trying, then our homes must be worth the dying.

Life and Inspiration

BY DAVID P. CARLSON

Inspiration is something that comes without an official announcement. Catapulted by either a personal or world event the subject unfolds in flight, then sails furiously to the ground. The trick is in the landing—the landing is the inspiration that God has charted – a safe and prosperous adventure from the take-off to the hangar.

Life Held Golden

BY DAVID P. CARLSON

Look, a child held still in a golden frame—he seems so
blue, so true—maybe innocence covers his face.

His stare calls us to remember when he had no sin.

In time he sees; his dark eyes flash with life. His
body moves, his soul stands never changing.

His portrait tells his story. His parents tell of his life—
his pain lies within him. His childish face leaves no
trace—leaves no hint of why he changed in time.

Lofty

BY DAVID P. CARLSON

Upon my cloud in the sky of life my tempered taste seems satisfied
by a candle's light in which my eyes have fixed a path. But the storms
of life and their seasons grow forever tense, forever longer through
the surging rage of time; passing years breed collected duties till the
sky is filled with lighted kites which all string neatly back to me.

So the task of life must have such burdens, but the
burdens of life cannot be my only task;
For the light I seek has a candle's glow; and its stringless
tie to my searching mind, is its salvation.

Looking Down into the pit I Stumbled Into Fifty Years Ago

BY DAVID P. CARLSON

Ca-choo—my lasting breath—all in one—my life
stands still, my eyes lay open and still. Pray, call out?
Throw my life's despair on stronger limbs?
Be merciful in my deliverance, cast down my robe of death,
be merciful in my sight. Oh, how long have I to wait?—how
long does mercy last before I die? I plead one lasting gift, just
one. Break down the walls of mercy and deliver me once more
another world to wring my face and shed one lasting tear.
All hail those who stands before me, for
they speak truths venom's blood.
BEGINNING THE AWAKING FROM THE DREAM.
How weekly I slur my words, how sweetly I whine. Is not this true
in this world we live? Sainted cares live only in our own bewildered
minds. What are cares which have only one beginning, one end?
Spare me such a tattered role in such a dismal play, leave me to grant
my wish— Oh, thine is so unworthy—a care, a feeling a part of
one's own soul, are they not worthy thoughts? In hell they leave me
not even an ash, not even one speck of light, they go not there.
So why can't I be in heaven where one knows such worth. Why?
Because I am here, we are here, we are in hell. Our lives are myths,
a fool's bewildered mind. There are those who remember, but not in
a memory's way. Could it be I say? Have I found a curse I dare not
know? God help me if I have. Is this one step down? Or two, or three?

Where are we in time, have we lived and died, lived and died, given
another chance in lines, in rows, down, down, down till we moan
in gutters, gasp for breath, hold our sides and scream. All hail thee
something—squeeze me one last time, for in the next life I will be
born in hell itself. HALF REALITY TRANSCENDS THE NIGHT.
THE FIRST NIGHT IN JAIL I feel the sweat, I feel
the cell, I cast my head down in the night and realize
I've been here an eternity engulfing three hours.
It's night, my first night, my only night in jail since I was conceived.
Then I remember—there was a year, a whole year, that no one can
tell me about, say about, nothing about that year. Maybe this is not
my first, my real mother, (whoever you are, were maybe now), I don't
know,--maybe she was in jail while I lay asleep within her. Could it
be? Imagine a whole year passing from Dearborn, Michigan, to San
Antonio, Texas, (where I was adopted) and not a hint of how or why.
The thoughts has always left me unknowing, wondering and making
excuses for those who cast me out. The wondering comforts me at
last, for only such a thought could now when my adopted mother
sleeps peacefully at home, not aware her son's soul leans slowly toward
times guillotine death. The tortures I bring march to her closer and
closer with every second, and with the morning, the day looks cheerful
to her. Now down to her daily tasks, and still the marching comes
closer. The tromping, (she surely heard in the distance of her dreams)
thundered on. The hum grows to a devastating peak, then the bugle
sounds and the blade lays bloody, cursed and abandoned. I FEEL
HER MOAN, I FEEL IT ALL, I CRY AND GASP A BREATH.
That morning, that slashing morning I knew my mother was died.

I WHIMPER HUMBLY, I WANT TO RISE AND GO CRY OUT
AT HER GRAVE, BEG A PRAYER TO HER, FOR HER,—but
I cannot, I am in jail. I cannot go, I must sit and think. Where is
glory at the moment you destroy all possibility of a normal life?
There hidden I suppose, also hidden in the rubble is the definition
of glory, all wrapped up in each of us. So the morning came, the
blade fell and the cries brought a stable mood and the mood in time
was bearable as is with repetition, repetition of the same thoughts
over and over until all thoughts are thought, all lives are hit and
we all attempt to stagger to reality and resume our former forms.
RECALLING THE MORNING I THOUGHT WAS A BAD
DREAM, THEN REALIZING ITS REALITY. The door opens,
(breakfast in hell). In lines we wait, we eat, for we must live even
though we live for nothing (just to live for the sake of living must
hunt men's souls). Silently we trudge forward and then we sit, we
feast, we whimper, we gag on our descendants gaze. Here we are,
grounded as a family of thieves, drunkards, smugglers, and all of us
slaves of our neglect, all neglected, all purified by distant thoughts
of a peaceful time. Such an hour in such a crowded mist and in it all
time stands blurred, not awake, but partly, then more, then more. Ah,
yes, I remember now, - O, God, I thought it was just a bad dream I'd
waken from and say, man that sure was a bad scene, but the dream
has just begun and you know it after about the third gulp of greasy
coffee, (thrown in as a luxury, but really as an awake call to the hell
we live). The mumbling of savage men (like bombs you hear far away)
reassure my awaking. Too soon your ears, your eyes and all sensations
quiver with life and all defense mechanisms lay slain by reality.

MORNING JAIL

The morning sun rises slowly with essence as its name. Like Satan himself, he bears down, rays drooping in like benefits from hell, (cordial openings for boiling water). I soak in heated swirls only the devil could have stirred so swiftly. Sweat pours from every pore and every breath proceeds thoughts wound in gloom, physical and mental yokes all harnessed in the seclusion of this cage I live. I think maybe sleep will rescue me from this day but such a trip would take too long and on what mobile thought, from what source of power could propel with enough thrust to drive me to oblivion from reality's stinging heat from body and soul? No chance of a Buddhist's trance or a switch to be turned off when thoughts rage out of control,- so the battle of sane and sanity pants on. So I keep thinking and now I realize,- go ahead and think you can't win- and the moment I stop fighting I realize, I snap, I think I must do anything of the smallest torture. Let's see—REMEMBERING THE ARREST IN LAREDO last night we were so screwed, so fiendishly clever to hide those four bulging sacks in the innocent looking wheel with the devil-may-care stamped clearly on each lug nut. I realize now how obvious it was that all of the other wheels were innocently dirty except the one left front tire, and that's what the man said, "just take off the left front tire and bust it down Mack." – and there it was. That guy at the service station didn't care. He was just making fifty cents to take the tire off. If he only knew what he was doing.
So there I stood partially in shock partially mindfully sane.
WHAT DID I DO? WHO? WHAT? I'VE EATERN
WHILE ASLEEP BUT WHAT HAVE I EATEN? I'VE
EATEN WHAT THEY GAVE ME, THEY GAVE ME
NOURISHMENT, BUT WHAT SHOULD THEY CARE.

Then it begins, I remember everything, not quite everything,
but enough. All these men, they are all Mexicans—I don't
care, but who will I explain to, who will understand, who will
care? In it all I'd forgotten my friends where here too. I took
in and out, over and around till, Hah! There they are—
In one breath I let out a sick sort of laugh gush out as I see JB sitting
there like Humpty Dumpty slaughtering a big old sweet roll. I wonder
about that. How could he be so hungry, like he didn't even notice he
was in jail. I seem to be expecting at any moment for him to finish his
rolls and reach for his coffee, sipping it slowly as his eyes fall on his
surroundings. Then he slowly lowers his cup, sets it softly on the metal
table and turns slowly looking at the horrible sight—then jumps to
his feet, holds his head and yells, "Hey, Man, What in the Hell?", but
none of this, he seems at home here—Oh, well, with a few more quick
glances I spot Terry sitting there like in a trance. He must be thinking
about anything but food. Such guessing is agony. If I'm tempted to
read minds, I have many other interesting, deep morals, code, answers
and lies to probe into right here before me. At least forty men, all
outcasts in their own ways, convicted by other laws more subtle than
those that put them here. But so much for sidetrack now. A span of
time must be paved by a laboring mind, (mine most assuredly) and I
am ready. Bold statements make the humblest of men seek refuge.

LAREDO TURMOIL

THE DREAMS FILLS MY CONSCIOUSNESS,-I snap, I crawl, I look up and study my surroundings-and then I a rise and wash my face. It was such a beautiful day too. I even felt good again after such a long, gasping, humble pleading, not pleading, but wondering, not wondering,--such an ordeal. I can't even seem to put my finger on the smallest muttering of my meager thoughts. Values seem trivial compared to my confusion. From the love of life to its trials, my paths have engaged in their own public stages. All who watch feel glorified by my witnessing. I have sinned before the eyes of man—now the shattering of lives and thoughts have subsided and sunk to the bottom—To them they feel rewarded and proud to sit in rose-tinted pulpits of purity for their pasts are far behind. REMEMBERING THE REALITY THAT BRINGS THIS STATE, THIS MIND relieved—Now I descend to and have descended from (what seems years ago, but really a month ago) that day not long ago in Laredo when the sacrifice to the guns of life (the sacred pigeons which fly above and protect our worldly goods but have not the wisdom to protect our trivial gloomy pleasures, thoughts, personalities and all that consisting of all things) were made public reality—Yes, sacrificed we were and the sacred pigeons' ears tingled to hear our gasps. (ADVANCING TO THE PAST "HELL" SURFACE AND DEEP THOUGHTS OF JAIL). In jails all over the world mountains of waste crap oozes on concrete floors, sweat from fallen men trickles from their hands and these beads of life shine the bars, reflect a human face before he leaves and trudges back to another spot, no so sad, not so gay—just a place called destination in such shrunken world. For your cage has limitations—you know them in a day, maybe hours considering your individual complexes. Laughing men having fun seems old here, children, skies, horizons, hills, these values increase as a minute's value becomes your cell and these hours of minutes heat your body and work you unmercifully (poems rage wildly DREAMING THE PAST HELL) and you think your lines and believe then, your memory retracts before the pigeons landed and what would you should or shouldn't have done appears in minds for escape. But the door is shut, and you slam into it trying to defy the gates of time but always too late. This gate is closed, never to be open again. (Never try this door unless you are a lover of endless torment)—I speak to myself of course, for minds everywhere are different and some agree just to be agreeing and some rebel just to be rebelling, but all are individual even though thoughts appear as twins.—Not so in essence, in essence is purity. Wandering in that land, you never expect to visit, I've always wondering what it would be like to get busted and now I know. Stop wondering, you fool, you'll have plenty of time to know even more. I didn't even have my shoes on—yeah there I was, busted barefooted. He fits the part, I bet they said, and JB with his beard and Terry talking fast looking, thinking and realizing, to no avail. He fits too and we all fit; we all were in our places. Carry on, carry on, keep thinking, now I think all that hurts and I don't care. It's all so insane, maybe because I'm going that way. The morning sun keeps rising and grows more heated with the debates—the morning. So I walk a short stroll to the long room where we ate earlier and to seek relief from the heat from forty men and exposed windows from one sun, a sun I once loved for its natural beauty and the color it cast at dawn and later when it sinks on another world, and I could see the edge dip to darkness, the span it left behind I loved, every day was a new world, every day held a promise of new awareness. Is it worth it now? All I want is oblivion, nothing more, complete silence, complete unawareness, complete simplicity of nothingness to roam through my being and forget to care, forget to understand, to quit seeking values higher than the grave we live in. I reached to stop his vision, to retreat this vomiting of a reeling mind.

It seems too late now. I want to see through darkened eyes eternity, death's eternity. I argue for life's side, I hold and shake till I listen, slap myself and say, listen! Shut up!! Time is your escape, wait till you see the sun setting just for you, pick a flower and see its colors with new eyes. Man understands limits, earthquakes, bombs, and stop—signs. So much more is there. Oh, when will it end? It ends only in your mind, two months, three months. Your values will stand ever brighter by this experience. I HANG LIMPLY FROM THE CAGER BARS AND CRY SOFTLY NOT WANTING TO BE SEEN. FINALLY, SOMEHOW I FIND STRENGTH SOMEWHERE TO BREATHE DEEPLY AND STOP THINKING ABOUT ANYTHING FOR OR AGAINST ANY. I FIND SLEEP FINALLY, NO DREAMS, NO NOTHING, JUST PEACEFULL SLEEP THROUGH ALL THE SWEAT AND MUMBLING. LIFE WON THIS TIME, BUT I KNOW SECLUSION FROM FREEDOM WILL WIN A MENTAL DEATH IF HELD TOO LONG. THE CONCLUSION OF THE SECLUSION

The morning sun rises slowly with essence as its name, like Satan himself, he bears down—rays droop in like benefits from hell—cordial openings for boiling water. I soak in heated swirls only the devil could have stirred so swiftly. Every breath proceeds thoughts would in gloom, physical and mental yokes all harnessed in the seclusion of this cage I live. (In 1953 THE SPIRIT OF GOD DREW ME OUT OF THE PEW), God drew me out of the pew, into the aisle and down to accept my Lord's salvation. I don't remember what Rev. Lunsford said, but I'll never forget the joy of that small, small boy. I received my crown, salvation's prize, but in the years to come, I believed a lie. I received my crown, but refused the sword that fights right and all sin abhors.

THE WORD OF GOD and THE HOLY GHOST, the very things I needed most, I laid aside, then bore the cost. It wasn't long and I forgot His name and only remembered when it was used in vain. My teenage years had come and gone that night the man said "Here's the phone, one call is all you get." 1966 was a dreadful year, void of joy, void of cheer. To view my life was hard to bear—my parents cried and the world denied any hope for such a boy. One night I wrote the words I quoted first and cried inside from bitter thirst, for the Word of God and the Holy Ghost. After 13 years in Babylon, I kneel'd down low beneath the load of wild life oats which I had soan, and on my knees I said, "Oh, please, Please, dear Lord, take me home." God heard that prayer from this lost sheep and began to guide my stumbling feet. How he did it I'll never know, but I'll never forget there on that road, that night I stumbled in form Babylon. Jerusalem's lights were as the floods of joy that I once knew as a small boy, so many years ago. God brought me back from hell on earth to share His word through the Holy Ghost, and though I live by his abundant grace, and behold all joy in Jesus' face—and though my foot's on solid ground and my eyes look up and never down— still the past of hell on earth, yet lives within the ones I hurt— CHRISTS SALVATION AS IT BEGINS, SHOULD CONTINUE ON TILL THE VICTORIES END, BUT WITHOUT GOD'S WORD AND THE HOLY GHOST—WELL, LOOK WHAT HAPPENED TO ME DOWN THE ROAD TO BABYLON.

Lord, It Ain't So Bad

BY DAVID P. CARLSON

Weeds and Vines and trees a-dying, carefully I unearth
their remains---balling and crying, hurting and lying.
Some people think living and dying is just the
same—but I've found a new refrain—
When I see dark, I see the Light;
When I see gray, I turn and pray and I say, "Lord, it ain't so
bad, no it ain't so bad"—carefully I unearth the remains.
Four score and ten from the beginning to end,
"Lord, it ain't so bad"; knowledge creeps in along the
ground—hopes and hobbies further down—no strength
to strike the crusted soil, only shadows in the brain remain
to exclaim, "Lord, it ain't so bad, no it ain't so bad".
How far is the horizon? How high the mountain peaks
they're on? How deep must we dredge to find the strength
to search among the remains, careful not to disturb the
resting place of something more than memories past; and
once again, "Lord it ain't so bad, no, it ain't so bad".

Machiavellian

BY DAVID P. CARLSON

While diligently and furiously depending on the continual onslaught of the slaughtering of helpless citizens, these world-class shroud-cladded, shadow-faced aristocrats join together to count the days when they might cunningly escalate those measly murdered few to a thousand-thousand, all to merge on time to be enriched for a mere donation of their sacrificially staged parading on those holy grounds of a multitude of plasma screens for propaganda's sake, to solidify for all of this their common goal to control the frightened, afraid and terrified. Headlines scream the pain of the slain today in Bible study, children slaughtered while at play, twelve more tragically have been gunned down in their own home town's resting place, their local majestic movie house complex arcades—some beheaded in plain sight, in perfect view on the evening news—others suffering, laying wounded behind the walls of our nation's malls or super grand sports arenas, bowling alleys and maybe even nursing homes. What is it that brings to this regimen of men (or just a simple ordinary soul) such joy to kill and maim his fellow man? Could it be as simple as a sub—or conscious plan to be a world-famous celebrity, to be flagged by a rag-tag professor, doctor, governmental or clinical physiological team who loves to write about such things –such as the criminal politically challenged sociopaths, and how their minds derive their train of thought down those broken tracks so soon to be detailed on some holy grail, to then to eventually be deemed insanely zealous of what they believe to be a holy tenet of some supreme life form, being Allah, Buddha, maybe Socrates or the Dalai Lama, and then to be analyzed, personified and finally understood to be the product of their own schizophrenic mental quest to reach that emblematic emboldened status of supreme martyrdom;

Now this highly educated examining team just simply notes him or them to have contracted a highly contagious social disease easily eradicated by a wholesome dose of therapy: Now about this their convoluted grand desire for ethnic cleansing of the human race, well that, of course, was brought about by Mom and Dad, or someone else they depended on that sadly let them down, or maybe it's this nation's Laws and Rights he or they love to trample on. Nevertheless they seem to all agree, "It's really just our educated guess". I guess that's why it will take so long to scotch their rumors of the impending annihilation of Christendom.

Now because of all this chaos we all take part for all can see how common sense can spark a super-sonic spending spree for buried bunkers, just the place to store the family's picture album, Gatling guns, rocket launchers and machetes: then up we go to the great outdoors to take a tour through the fields of orange, peach and apple trees, there to pick a few for a tasty snack while the kids and neighbors scurry far and wide to find some rocks and bricks to help build the moat around their castle's towering walls, sturdily built over six feet thick so there to hide and house their tanks and trucks abundantly stocked with poison gas and booby traps, just in case they might run across some of those roving bands of zombies, Nazis, or gypsy clans who may decide to invade the land.

But with all of this, our well-planned defense, all is never really ever well, for you can always tell with a single glance the face behind the mask Beelzebub, the Antichrist, there to proclaim a truce to take us all away to that promised land to place a noose around our necks, and there to be introduced to his Sharia lawlessness.

Truth is, "the soul that sinneth shall surely die, "physically and that highly debated spiritual side. Now all of this life on earth has stirred mankind so that he has reached his final apogee, so much farther away from that heavenly bond than could ever have been imagined, others so near to that heavenly perigee, better known as that moment shown as when God lets you know you're not alone, so near you'll hear him whisper "Welcome home, be of good cheer, I have overcome this world's shrouded, shadowed-faced aristocrats whose common goal is to control with hate (their favorite tool), the terrified and alone. But, when I come sayeth the Lord, they will be the ones to cringe in fear behind their closet doors—once again my chosen friends, my begotten ones—fear not, we all will overcome by enduring to THE END.

Matador, Picadores, and the Bull—El Picayune

BY DAVID P. CARLSON

Circling; taunting the mysterious picayune creature upon the ground
El picador plots another painful jab. From on high, astride his prancing
beast, el picador feels compelled to take the call on his red and yellow
vibrating cell of a phone. What a time to be disturbed when life
and death are on the line. (No pun intended). Now peering over his
tree trunk boarded barricade El Matador prepares for his dramatic
entrance dance. After a little pirouette he stumbles into the bull's
domain to claim the life of El picayune, the sacrifice for a cheering
few. Oddly enough, the bull seems calm as El Matador scrambles
around to find his sword, his cape and one tennis shoe. Finally when
all his paraphernalia has been returned from the grand arena's "lost
and found" he again emerges from the wings, this time half dressed
with sword in hand and a silly grin to attack that beast in a fit of
rage; then cries "I'll kill your hide even if it be with my own bare
hands!!", but just in time the bull, he steps aside and gores El Matty in
both hip and side, and on top of that, he tore his pants. That's when
Matty screamed out for Picador and his boys and said, "you need
to stab this bull a few more times if I'm gonna do the crime." Well,
when that didn't work out so good, old Matty just pulled out his gun
and shot that bull, then went his way to flight again another day.
Well, the moral or the lesson I'm guessin' is, if you're gonna
fight the Devil and his crowd on his own turf, don't wait till
he pull's a gun; just gore him where it will do some good; then
take his sword and his cape, and as he turns and limps away
call him Picayune Paltry, or with an old Webster's English
definition it might be better said—"Oh, ye of little worth!!"

Monastic Wind—Inane Branches

BY DAVID P. CARLSON

Green and thin now equates to trembling lusts of chlorophylling gel within the veins of leaves from their long extended stems and branches. The relentless gusts of winter's breath bends then twists till all seems lost, all is tossed from side to side till the wind collides, buckles and then subsides again. Motionless, the limbs silently weep and groan, as the tear-like sap flows from those countless leaves and splintered twigs they once caressed (but now sadly are bereaved) as their seed-rich stems, all now strewn and broken upon the ground, then seized by God, there to be whisked away by another late December breeze. The wind; your friend or foe? Oh, but for sure a force to be reckoned with—Consult the forest, consult the Lake and all that is therein. Death and Life both consort to move ahead—so march they do in one accord, in lock and step their steady stride; so they do and carry on in unison until they both receive the call, the commander's loud resounding cry "Halt!, stand at ease, now kindly step aside." Now stiff and straight the limbs of death and life stand as one shivering there in the airless damp dark abyss. With a blustery gush, the wind picks up again to strive alive; again to carry them to their timeless quest to understand the power of the wind –but without the air life and death remain secure. As the wind subsides the serenity of it all sets them both adrift. The wind, the force in every death, in every life merely withdraws those cloistered chlorophyll-filled stems of life from deep within man's futile attempts to show respect. Finally in their last of days the limbs can only gently sway and reluctantly break away. No more a place for tears to form and freeze, glistening as they dangle there upon the

branch of another winter day—the wind simply grins, then silently
slips away, leaves his monasterial cloist-er to grieve again another day.
Monastically, this cloistered wind miraculously transposes
nature's natural metamorphosis while swirling down to change
in form – oh so greatly now—flash the lightening—and as the
thunder trumpets his grand eternal transformation he reaches
out clutching all within his path amidst the clouds aloft, then
spiraling low to grasp the prey to control the swaying motions
of another set of inanimate branches along the way.
There are more than two, maybe more some summer days in which
the wind whips the limbs of your ever-growing contemplations. Some
of you thank the storm for controversies, some take the blunt of the
hurricane that rip your young and fragile saplings to the ground.
Howling or gently flowing this carousel-like wind is forever in control
of our every goings and all of our abatings. But in the ever-looming end
of life's seasons, life will spring forth her light to at last reveal the loving
face of God, and there again the force of life, his ever present Wind.

Never Ending Rain

BY DAVID P. CARLSON

Among the clouds the moisture hides within those towering
chambered walls, content to ride the rising heat to meet the cold
and frigid air aloft, to spawn therein the warmth wherein she
hibernates—while on earth her friends, the trees, the plants,
the grass all gather there to germinate, waiting patiently for the
rumbling thunder behind the flash of lightening strikes to flush
the sky of her abundant rain on those starless and windy nights.
As drops of rain, each tear in life is loosed on high to fall, then
grace the sky with the scented incense essence of a human kind of
kindness, a trait once held sublime; destined tears (that plunge as
streaks to meet the earth on those cloudy sunless days), spill their
lives for that hope that man, that wife and child may come to
realize the price of love; so that they might sup, then rise to grow
up tall, to shed the pain of their obdurate and fruitless lives.
So now, as their sublimeness has been regained they lift up their leaves
as an evening shower sprays the soil with early mourning-drops as
tears, to once again regerminate, then cultivate a new genetic strain
to reign and rhyme with the God who created the human soul and
mind – a soul designed to be revived by humankind, another kind
of sacrifice that leads to harvest time by his never-ending rain.

Ordinary Angle

BY DAVID P. CARLSON

"What can you spare my brother?" breathed the aged prophet
to the scribe. I'll tithe a farthing and a mite, never mind the
cost; but mind you, sir, all the silver and all the gold can ne'er
repair nor soothe the pain contained within this tomb of
hopes assumed as doomed, better known as mediocrities.
As the stench of despair is masked with a hint of mint and a dash
of authenticity, the aroma slightly impairs his sarcastic mood, but
still inspires the imprisoned scribe to print with feathered pen his
questions upon the wall—Am I without or am I within this united
state of mediocre; am I just another shell upon the sand in a land long
forgotten? Is this my day to be crowned with eternal anonymity, now
verging on the first stages of narcolepsy; "Really?" It may sound silly or
a bit insane to quibble about my quest in life, to seek a higher plain, to
labor in this sea of sand; but tell me, sir, from where you stand outside
this tomb, where have I gone astray or shall I begin again another day?
Once again breathed the prophet to the scribe, "What can you spare
that you might find or what portion will you be willing to cosign;
surely more than a farthing or a mite. Now, just pay your tithes, repent
and pray, then weigh your wages each and every day. Live for God who
sent His Son and know that nothing is ever deemed mediocre if God
receives from you at least his ten percent and, maybe, just a little over.

Pity

BY DAVID P. CARLSON

A graveyard empty. A man leans and picks a flower
for no one but himself; His name is pity—
His heart has no soul—He murmurs a lonely song
he memorized because he felt it was to him—
He knows nothing of what he does—He only thinks,
"if it were only like that I could be happy"-
He talks to lonely people—He speaks aloud to empty
rooms thinking someday he'll find someone to listen.
He writes a sad tale, then feels he's failed
to describe himself very well—
What will happen to a man like this? Find his way, find his heart?
Who will listen when all is said? Only no one. Only hell.

Salvation's Happy Days

BY DAVID P. CARLSON

Saints glide with me across blue-grey skies—
Pink roses garnish my hair as the wind ruffles the bellowing clouds—
I dance in horizons filled with hope.
Eyes reflect the glorious sight—
I reach for life with outstretched arms.
I behold sights fading, flicking deep upon my smiling face—
The branch of life sways in godly breaths—
Tender emotions sink from within starlit skies—
Darkness melts around me—
I fade into it another night, looking forward to another
day and another night to kneel and pray.

Soul Searchers

BY DAVID P. CARLSON

The truth spoken in corridors of lines, blended in the longing of life,
now kneel dented by the pressures of a wondering mind, speckled
with the experience of time, of situations so long forgotten but still
left suspended in the infancy of truth, or what seemed truthful.
To me sainted beliefs span as a shadow of a
wondering mind on landscapes of purity.
With this we breed years of gasping decisions.
I need the beliefs that someone has sometime needed one
blissful minute wrapped in one word spoken from the soul.

Summer Rain

BY DAVID P. CARLSON

A black framed screen again holds my portrait—through it I
see the violence of nature's emotions; flashing anger erupts.
The beauty I once found erupts—the beauty I once found, (cascading
in all its glory, seasoned glory) chills not one fiber in me.
There held in dark reverence, my life—rain drops barely heard,
raindrops hang the trees with tears—air rests silently—I hear my
heart like distant thunder—I find nature's violence within me—
My eyes flash surrender to summer rain.

The Arrow, the Archer, the Bow and String

BY DAVID P. CARLSON

The bow layered with gopher, shittim wood and cedar, stained and polished, shaped by time even before it started. Such a grand transformation of an array of past transactions; now with bow in tack the master archer begins to weave but a single strand of linen, twined with silk, woven without a seam, yet so thin and common as a single, simple ordinary string; he'll stretch it out to fit the bow when bent, now content to be the finial cord, he'll secure it tight and fast to the last belay, there to withstand the constant strain, oh so taut between the to-and-fro of the alpha and omega's poles. Now with bow in hand the master archer needs but one more precious item to be found and spent, a quiver full of only one straight and narrow armor-piercing arrow. This arrow now fit and feathered, now set and glued has but one more step to be tried and then approved, to be bound up tight, certified to be accounted sublimely worthy to be the shaft of life, to be laid upon the master's bow. With string set tight within the arrow's hasp the mighty archer draws back his bow, and with prey in sight (with one more belated breath) he lets the arrow go. You might say at that moment there in time, their was a greatly strained relationship between the archer, arrow string and bow. Rapprochement is the word I have in mind which simply means to me, a restoration of a once strained, then broken eternal tie with all mankind; now thanks be to God (the master archer) for the arrow lent, prepared for the flight, to forgive, so now to find its mark upon the heart of all the lives since time was derived. Such is our life we seek each day upon the bow and string, an arrow to be let go.

The Camel and the Fox

BY DAVID P. CARLSON

The camel and the fox, a peculiar pair; friends for life compelled to share their lives within the lion's lair. Computers sing a constant stream of information; but soon the camel shows his extremely strained and futile frustrations—"If only I were sly and quick so as to note what keys to click I'd order up a batch of tricks to trap that old fox, then save his tail to hang around my neck for my first trip to the "Casino Sands" there in Nevada's land. Now with some luck I'd win the cup, and then when I'd cashed in I'd pay the price and bisect these humps (though filled with life and nourishment) and trade them in for a trip to the Promised Land, in the land of the midnight sun. Now on my sleigh of six-foot wide, I'd wave goodbye to the Land of Sand and that old fox and his sarcastic grin. Now he would be the one with the lonesome gaze, left to trod the sand without a trail to sway from side to side. I would wish him luck but as it is, I'll retain my humps and just be me; that's just life you see—or do we; Ya know that old fox we desire to deceive just could be you and me from time to time, a dueling set of personalities. That old Camel, he seems slow ya know, kinda saunters around and feeds on grass and, "Hey!", he's just trying to get along. But that old fox, he's rude at times, his temper's quick and sometimes he's out of line. So let's just crank it back a bit and start this poem once again. Now for Mr. Camel and Mr. Fox to get along its gonna take a little time and a lot of help from two of man's best friends; Father God and his Son—the Word and the Chance they both get born again.

The Countess and the Beast

BY DAVID P. CARLSON

Searching secretly through the compost-destined
Mounds of political turmoil is the Mind-beast,
Patented and protected by the countless conspirators,
All courting the same Countess of Courtesy,
Veiled in her transparent gown,
Naked and exposed to her own opaque arrogance,
That gropes through her endless array of deceptive attires—
"Politically correct" yet completely disconnected from
All her common interests that once was "Life and Liberty",
And now she comfortably lies in the lap of all her comforters
While frolicking in the mire of her deceptiveness—
This Mind-Beast, Father to all compulsions,
Now truly is perfidy and totally incoherent to the masses.
His mind-set is totally dedicated to his objectives
And now to us all is obviously oblique to all his surroundings
Of smoking mirrors and shouting orators.
Now hand-in- hand the Countess and the Beast in lockstep
Precision march down this stained-glass road
Where eternity's light will never shine,
Politically correct in every way,
But in his house his mirrors have forever denied his kind,
For never a reflection can ere be seen,
Because of his own opaque-crusted mind,
The Countess and the Beast now need another site
To speak their wedding vows,
Where eyes and ears are mute and blind,
Where Hate and Death can truly rhyme
Outside the sight of Truth and Love—
Transparency of another kind can only wait
By Faith, on the Others Side.

The Dark Ages

BY DAVID P. CARLSON

Behind thine eyes lies a brain—complicated and confused—
Through precious sight we breed pure-bred knowledge
of our surrounding to this mind-beast—pollened
and spermed by every fathering moment.
Dry brown limbs crackle, crack silently as puppets for silent winds.
Beetles, Crickets, all small crawling things
scurry as men beneath sequoia forests.
Their world of living phenomena is as our own. The dark Ages in
miniature is their environment and truly must be their own.
A scream, a shout, rumbling motors, wailing whistles, blasts
from guns, all are but echoes from the human world above.
Brisk winds- forest's noises, the switch and crash of falling
dying limbs are as the beginnings, the dark ages.
Night descends with the passing light-wind clutch-hold still clear
nights- upon dark-blue velvet skies sparkle lights of years before. Dark-
green spouts of emerging youth hang face-down in absents of the wind.
Then the rumble in the heavens- a flash of light turns green
emerging youth- a gust of moist autumn rain shines her
surface—propels her motions with stormy violence.
Young green grass spouts dance with new emotions, whips
in autumn's breath, damp with seasons tear—
Beside emerging youth, the old and dying and the dead.
Storm clouds move, then chatter in the distance—
A full moon looms in hazy patterns behind the basking clouds—
A barking dog barks the night into silence, leaves a green grass sprout
crying tears upon a dark-brown grave, in miniature even prayed.

The Gray Day

BY DAVID P. CARLSON

Through misty fog waters, unshined space, the appearance of
gray is conceived without power of thought and reasoning.
The gray of a dawnless day flows into the cavities
of the mind like hot lead into its mold.
But why is such a flow standard to more than half?
Cannot it be conceived as in between bliss from dark and brilliance,
A peaceful inheritance of blended thoughts cradled
in the cool damp rival of dominant colors.
So it is for me.

The Jasmine of the Night
Cestrum Nocturnum

Cestrum nocturnum (common names include night-blooming jasmine, night-blooming cestrum, lady of the night, queen of the night, night-blooming Jessamine, and Hasnuhana (Bengali:is a species of cestrum in the plant family Solanaceae (the potato family). It is native to the West Indies but naturalized in South Asia.

Night-blooming jasmine is an evergreen woody shrub growing to 4 meters (13 ft) tall. The leaves are simple, narrow lanceolate, 6-20 in) centimeters (2.4-7.9 in) long and 2-4.5 centimeters (0.79-1.77 in) broad, smooth and glossy, with an entire margin. The flowers are greenish-white, with a slender tubular corolla 2-2.5 centimeters (0.79-0.98in) long with five acute lobes, 10-13 millimeters (0.39-0.51 in) diameter when open a night, and are produced in cymose inflorescences. A powerful, sweet perfume is released at night. The fruit is a berry 10 millimeters (0.39 in) long by 5 millimeters (0.20 in) diameter, the color of an aubergine. There is also a variety with yellowish flowers. There are mixed reports regarding the toxicity of foliage and fruit.

The Jasmine of the Night

BY DAVID P. CARLSON

The moon arrives in its iron cage, the lock, is snapped, then thrust aside. This nocturnal mother –of-pearl breaks through the silence of the night to emerge from behind that rainforest's golden doors; a time to shine in this place where truth and lies collide, to blossom once again by the power of her moonlight hour, this jasmine of the night.

The Jasmine of the Night

BY DAVID P. CARLSON

The moon arrives in its iron cage, the lock, is snapped, then thrust
aside. This nocturnal mother –of-pearl breaks through the silence of
the night to emerge from behind that rainforest's golden doors; a time
to shine in this place where truth and lies collide, to blossom once
again by the power of her moonlight hour, this jasmine of the night.
A perfect place for this poem to have found its end, but still this
cestrum nocturnum flower has scarce but one night, one life to unfold
her greenish paragon of inflorescence beauty from deep within; then
sadly destined there to fade and shrivel, as to once again succumb to
the brilliance of God's relentless sun, to evaporate her sweet perfumed
fragranced dew from up off her long solicitous and solemn leaves for
another continual ending of her nocturnal space of grace, so marked
by a quick retreat into her hibernated, reclusive state, so forlorn.
Now surging through her withering stems and blossoms, there
still flows a divine desire from God alone, a cherished goal to
bare her soul before a greater light, there to display her truth, to
deny the lie that life and death can coexist within the gloom of
this dark abyss we call the night, there beneath the fog of this
diminished moonlight glow—this lesser light so caged and locked
can only now recent his claim on the jasmine families name
"Solanaceae"—for now to his chagrin this flower blossoms only
for one greater light within, the one that grants to her the right to
live and bloom once again, in a land where there is no night.
So is the promised hope for the jasmine of the night, to forgive,
then bloom and blossom within the sight of the living God,
never to have her beauty hid, but forever displayed, arranged
and named by God himself as his sweetly savored bouquet
delight, the now transformed, "Jasmine of the Light".

The Parachute

BY DAVID P. CARLSON

We live in times of war on distant shores, yet war is all around us;
The currents of life swirl in the pools of our own glass-cast aquariums
as the signs of the times flicker upon the walls and screens before
our eyes, then die to dreams in our dark unconscious hours.
Death and Greed (spawned by transparent seeds, split by ancient
Cain and his descendants) beckons us from the blackened coals of
burned out trees in the deep beyond below, "Proceed, proceed"—
Is this the cliff time has prepared for all mankind? Over and down,
through such a massive cloud of emptiness, we need not fear to
go. If only we could procure a handy parachute, to then regain
control of life's destined plans to purge our precious atmosphere
of the air we share; then, and only then, can we gently settle down
without a war to mar the ground, our final resting place.
That parachute, of course, is the Christ who beckons us with His
loving voice, "Proceed, Proceed"; rest in peace with Me—
"For without Me, you can do nothing."

The Turtle and the Skunk

BY DAVID P. CARLSON

Weird from here within this cave I bravely huddle in—I mean
the light, the way it streams in, then flickers upon this maze of
darkened corners, then jerks, then dances across the floor, then
seems to disappear up and down through those cavern's corridors,
then once again the darkness reaches in to close the door, thus sets
me free to confront the sounds of alley cats, mice and rats clawing
through through a plethora of tin trash cans full of discarded foods
and toys—Like music to my ears, this symphony of disconcerting
abstracts all colliding, then come tumbling in like glass on pots and
pans to one colossal crescendo before the end—Just another day
within this turtle shell, my cardboard hell—oh well—Hey, what's
that scratching on my shell, pray tell—oh, yeah, my friend, the
skunk; he visits me from time to time to remind me there's another
world out there—yeah, the one I fled in 2012—that's why I've come
to this alley home to where I have now resigned to forever dwell--
-so now my goal is to escape from that old skunk I call my oracle
or reality: I fell compelled to yell—" Hey, mate, what's going on
out there?"—slowly I may, as turtles may someday, emerge from
this cardboard box to again befriend that old skunk.(You may
prefer to infer he should be addressed as my over-rated sanity).
It would be nice to shed this shell and walk upright again,
but then the question that will still arise is, "Why?"

But then the answer came, to my surprise, that old skunk was in disguise. His true identity was the angle of the truth, void of lies and vain deceit. The stench I smelled was not the skunk, but was all those lies I'd buried there deep within those caverns beneath this cranium shell I call my mind, that say there is no hell, no heavenly paradise in which to dwell—no earthly test that we must pass to overcome to hear God say, "Well done my son, enter in "—The only reality I once embraced was my own oblivious state that denied the truth there within my laminated cardboard case—now if I may, I do repent and shed this shell of hate for a crown of life and two good wings to fly above this earthen pond up to the gate where heaven waits to give a hug and welcome in, Both the turtle and skunk.

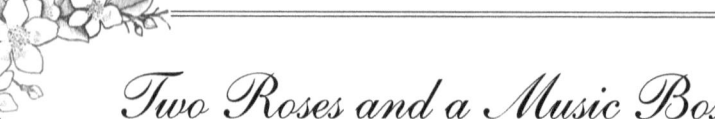

Two Roses and a Music Box

BY DAVID P. CARLSON

(Christ's prayers and flowers—God's chimes in times of trouble)

Two roses and a music box, two hearts one simple song.
I pray, my dear, that your unborn tears will never be shed
alone; but if someday as roses may, you lose some petals in a
summer storm, then take these works or these chimes or this
heart of mine and shine a rainbow through your tears;
The day in the life of a rainbow bright, how brief the light
of her life. The memory of her gaze on that bright but rainy
day, to me will be a sea of green and gold, so as the light from
the dawn bends shadows along the pathways of your mind,
let the green and the gold beneath the rainbow's bow be the
treasure of your soul--- so take these words or these chimes or
this heart of mine and shine a rainbow through your tears.

Vertig—the Illusion of Euphoria

(The family reunion of Vertigo, Euphoria Grandeur and Illusion with Family Friend, Johnny Pride—The Adventure)

BY DAVID P. CARLSON

Back flip into the icy blue, his tanks filled up to the brim by a slight of hand, a massive dose of vertigo. Tumbling down to what his mind thinks is up, he goes higher into the depths below, there to swim in the illusion that sharks and fools are his potential friends with whom he prefers to roam—but truth can plainly see he swims along alone. Now sinking into the abyss (that he mistakenly viewed as the path to abysmal blessedness) he sees emerging from beneath the grandeur mountain peaks his manifesto request, written and approved, his task assigned for him to climb the icy slops of Mt. Illusion to the grandeur that he seeks.

Just in time, slithering up from the heights below his beautiful sea-green creature friend, Queen Euporia. On her back he'll hitch a ride to the base camp on the other side of Mt. Grandeur and there he'll prepare to climb. He'll pack a meager lunch of tasty crumbs and don his wares with camel humps (another tank of what he thinks is air) and then from there he'll scale those daunting peaks below.

There he'll scroll there on that sandbar shoal "My NAME is Johnny Pride" and on this peak I'll stake my claim to be the greatest orator and adventurer ALIVE: but then to his dismay he sees the arrogance in his twisted LIE—had spelled it wrong,--and now etched in stone his claim to fame now begins to erode, then to wash away from the sandstone shallows of his brain, the residue of vertigo. As an ocean surge he rises up once more to say—my name is now Johnny Shame, and my erratic acts I do deduce my best excuse is my highly impaired equilibrium.

Exhausted, confused, and bruised; now sprawled there flat upon his back he finally clearly sees the illusion of euphoria has no grandeur to attract—with one last gasp he finds his breath, the reaches up to grasp the love and mercy in God's hands, but this time without his gloves. Now Grace and Faith soar as one to restore his will to breathe and live again firmly upon his raft above. From there he'll journey up to the shore do dine with God, sip from the cup of Life and Love with Him forevermore. The grandeur man has been looking for a last, alas the perfect metaphor has now made clear, there is no vertigo with God; with God the way is always UP, his directions always SURE.—AMEN

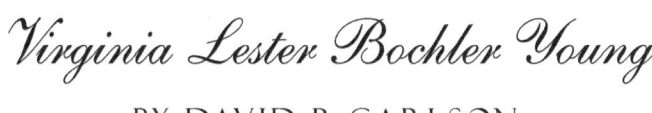

Virginia Lester Bochler Young

BY DAVID P. CARLSON

The woman be my mother—Virginia Lester Bochler Young—her
past I know of none—her voice distant hum. Her face a ghostly
place within my mind—Virginia Lester Bochler Young.
Twenty-five years and eight months ago, I know I hurt some. She
gave life, yes, Lester's wife—Virginia Lester Bochler Young.
Was it rainging the night I was born, Mother?
Was lightening striking, Mother? The Night I was
born, was the wind howling down the streets there
in Dearborn town, the night I was born?
Was Lester waiving in the hospital hall, Mother?
Was he sitting down or doing the town—and wishing I were dead?
How I must have burdened you that cold and dreary night Mother.
Well, as of this day, I've wedded twice and not one child was
born to me—for a child to me would be like a child in Virginia's
arms—a seed you planted well—Virginia Lester Bachler Young.

Vision

BY DAVID P. CARLSON

Is man is a mere version of the immaculate, eidetic creator, even
endowed with certain idiosyncrasies so as to be enjoined within
the incarnation of goodness yet to have an innate trait of evil,-
-thus among us the perverted versions, all yet to be converted?
Can a child be simply a product of genetic biological grafting
in that the mere essence of such a literary idiomatic joining (or
better said "God-sent") of these three separate entities, "sequence
of places", "time", and "events" simply to be viewed as inane or
even mundane occurrences, designed to populate the planet?
Flash a momentary flickering upon the screen that fluctuates,
so to be deemed by man weather to be sane or insane. The man
through nattily is mainly a multi-functional, yet mostly a singularly
focused species bent on dominating one and only one sphere of
a self-proclaimed characteristic, that of continual conjecture.
Now considering the isthmus between man and God, From vision
to version, now set a course, now not so blaringly ennui, but with
your heart in hand transcend and spin, career across those raging
streams and roaring rivers,--now join as one with both boat and
rider, crashing through those foaming rapids, smashing, lurching,
frantically searching, groping, clawing to grab those dangling vines
and drooping limbs from that rock embedded bank, so then to
subdue the relentlessness of this marching torrents raging toward
the impending waterfall of death, a fate of life's eternal end.
Oh, but remarkably sir, this master Olympic mariner of sorts, bravely
plunges headlong in with a fearless grin to swim upstream against
the tide, to then emerge with anchor dangling from his side to greet
the cheers of admiring fans he is now so rightly been endeared.

That manly version, now reclines, convalescing in the dark regions and reservoirs of his mind. Now coveting what he believes himself to be, that total package, the enigma man in combat mode, extinguishing all of life's istical infernos of fears from within his mind, but unknowingly he has been graphically implanted before a body of his peers; but amazingly he is still convinced there upon his cot of the veracity of his noble plight—but then the vision flickers once again upon the screen; time relents, colors fade as the isthmus between the vision and the version experiences a devastating, crippling and total collapse—so of course the vision of his creation sadly comes to rest at the conclusion of his course. No need to revise another profound infusion of another perverted version— That which comes from the original is an original in itself—but that which is perverted becomes a version—not the vision of the Creator.

Waiting in the Wings of the Final Hour: Chimera, Countess of Terror

BY DAVID P. CARLSON

Chimera awakened—this aristocracy-type of goat of sorts, snake-tailed, fire-breathing female, terror-breeding sociopath, far more than a mythical monster of Greek mythology—making up her face to deceive the minds of all mankind, while all the white this nation's pride has gone so sadly far astray, striding tirelessly over the edge of time's most awaited sacrosanctic hour, "The end of time", where ticks are replaced with judgments and tocks by multitudes of regrets, all slipping over the ledge into those crosswinds of cosmic space without limits, where limits are forever lost in an unlimited span of ornately painted vermillion sails, all so furiously driven by those solar winds of God's universal condemnation of Chimera's recreant fallen angels.

These antediluvian faces of past and present counters with cursings, sucking in with every breath her venom to then be injected into the protoplasm of demented men.

Chimera, this lioness of evil, this didactical professor of recalcitrance, her tail of ruby-studded sins, all engulfed by her vomiting flames within the solar plexus of men, always to be just one click away from many ephemerally inserted moments of "pshaw", then left to enjoy her rewards for wickedness from within the realm of this nations laws without reproach from this nation's moral codes of acronymic words, so disguised that no one can assume what's right or wrong, only what seems able to conform to fill empty gloom, surely right for at least one afternoon.

Chimera, the worlds' so-called last hope for an antidote to cure what she calls Christendom's prevaricated hope for divine immortality. So now there for all to embrace, a few alphabetically arranged collections of chimer's acrimonious thoughts, all contrived within the mind of who else, this anti-Christian caped-crusader, now waiting for her final fate, the prophetic conformation of a time no longer allowed to procrastinate or sit and ponder, now only silence just before that inviolable hour where once again Chimera hears, "The mysteries of God has been forever finished", thus saith the seventh angel of Revelation, Ten-six and seven.

Wind

BY DAVID P. CARLSON

The wind, the force in every death, in every life merely withdraws
those cloistered chlorophyll-filled stems of life from deep within Man's
futile attempts to show respect. Finally in their last of days the limbs
can only gently sway and reluctantly break away. No more a place
for tears to form and freeze, glistening as they dangle there upon the
branch of another winter day—the wind simply grins, then silently
slips away, leaves his monasterial cloist-er to grieve again another day.
Monasticallty, this cloistered wind miraculously transposes
nature's natural metamorphosis while swirling down to change
in form—oh so greatly now—flash the lightning—and as the
thunder trumpets his grand eternal transformation he reaches
out clutching all within his path amidst the clouds aloft, then
spiraling low to grasp the prey to control the swaying motions
of another set of inanimate branches along the way.
There are more than two, maybe more some summer days in which
the wind whips the limbs of your ever-growing contemplations.
Some of you thank the storm for controversies, some take the blunt of
the hurricane that rip your young and fragile saplings to the ground.
Howling or gently flowing this carousel-like wind is forever in control
of our every going and all of our abating. But in the ever-looming end
of life's seasons, life will spring forth her light to at last reveal the loving
face of God, and there again the force of life, this ever present Wind.

Winter's Land

BY DAVID P. CARLSON

At times love is beautiful—Love has many loves echoing in time;
beckoning to be had---
Souls filled with happy smiles, fade with winter's coming—
Green plagues empty rooms—Hope emerges, denies defeat--
Life stands clear through anxious waiting, then disfigures in
Sundown shadows—
Summer flows—Fall fails—Spring brings new love—Winter
howls surrender—
Lives wither as cold love numbs—
Hearts take love from within our hallowed dreams—sitting;
facing winter nights, night winds beckon—
Rain drops hang your face with tears—Human drops on human
skin take your warmth—leaves you clutching winter's hand—
warmth a precious thing when winter comes.
So now, solicitously I stand in winter's robe, clutching warmth
where I can. I reach to feel the cold might wind, Tears on winter's
face I touch, Her sadness holds me, clutching warmth where she
can. I take her hand, I understand—her tears splash, then turn to
ice. A winter's night has found a friend.

Within Us

BY DAVID P. CARLSON

Blue Skies—Red Skies—Tenderness;
Then love; Life darts within us—
Death kneels before us.
A sparrow fell yesterday—his lifeless form then turns
to ashes—His was a simple life—he was without sin.
He surely felt the pain of death—His death brought joy
to some small boy.
He was surely not a man!
Blue skies—Red skies
In heaven they felt the pain.

Youth Plight— Velvet Covered Antlers in the Snow

BY DAVID P. CARLSON

Consequences, the grand order of judgment; consequences, the perfect reward for obedient children from a loving and understanding creator. Now surely, surly is this juvenile/man, there left behind among those shining pines of this winter's testing grounds, there to wear those diamond-studded colored buttons upon his velvet-covered manly antlers, so deeply buried in the snow. Truly a novice so perfectly denotes his stature, truly naïve, reflects the pattern of his wanderings through the snow and ice-covered shoals.

There stretched upon his bed of definitiveness among the shrubs, tangled weeds and dangling thatches, he pounders the worth of his life-long conclusions that daily guide his way to that manly state of maturity. Complicated is his journey among the vines of daily-invoked rhetorically-framed hypothetical questions followed by streams of rapid-infested rivers of equally intimidating, if not discriminating choices of answers, all echoing through those cerebral canyon chasms of rock granite cliffs, so secludedly entombed within his own sub-degrees of ice and snow, that minute cluster of painful blisters are soon formed, so divinely packed within his frozen stare that then he sees the void of his own last days and there as well, with his mind impaired by his crippling mental hypothermia, he contradicts his prior pleas of mercy and equality there beneath the frozen grass and leaves of reality. Curiously those little winter birds inspect those velvet-covered antlers in the snow, then chirp and sail away through those flying crystal specks of glass like ice as they go there way. Now to there dismay those lifeless antlers shake as though still attached to some living creature's face, eyes and nose.

Then slowly there he gathers strength to stand and face the
sun's resplendent chromospheric glow—resurrection now
unfold for those velvet-covered antlers in the snow.
Such is our hope to avoid such tragic consequences of a youthful life
not yet fully followed through. Such is the gorge between the young
and the old and rightly so, for Father God and man. So unveil the
crimson velvet shroud from off those horns of God's eternal alter. The
battle waits; no room for doubt, no time left to falter—with cloak
in hand his youth unfurls this his velvet stained vermillion shroud,
left to dangle in shredded strips, dripping blood to the snow below,
exposed to all of this life's wildernesses of predatorial guests that
pause, then quickly stand to see this massive stag receive his granted
promise, his elegant crown of horns to rule the land, to fight and clash
with all that might attempt to mount his throne, to trample down
his well-deserved manly antlers held high above the melting snow.

Anthracite and Dexterous
A House and Buggy to Watch
for at the Finish Line

BY DAVID P. CARLSON

With dexterity shriveling and shredded youth enjoined within the
stiffening order, this fragile man with his demurring spirit now
dares to denounce their so-called promise of his predestinated,
inevitable, soon demise, so contrived within the eyes of his accusers.
Slanted are those rolling hills of a men's last days, also those projected
summits of each his aspirations, all then to be chronologically
enhanced, judged to be enigmatic, then sent spiraling outward
by those hostile blasts of distraught dissenters to the apogee of his
life's-long goals of extended youth (a true superlative of abundant
dexterity so desired by all mankind). This second wind, if you may,
to ascend within the realm of his own intense desire to fly upon the
wings of his antiquated antediluvian (yet for from obsolete) horse and
buggy body—to ignite to his delight his love for life and something
to look forward to in the last days of his anthracitical existence,
though so intense the heat, so low the flame, so minute the smoke,
all so designed to deny the complete unconspicuousness of it all.
Does this now sound as the sort of man that would resort to desperate
groping for cords within to secure a hand to hold or some convenient
notch to clutch among those jagged rocks of insecurity? Now, I say,
all of this I pray is to encourage his intentions to prevail beyond
allotted time before the eyes of his equally aged fellow-elders, to be
reborn and then rebounded with new dexterity within his human
mind's soulful core. Continually we shrivel and stiffen from life to
death, then to be revived again by uncoquettish and decorous spirits
in constant search for our diademed transcentdent such known as
the Giver of dexterous youth, the Alpha, the Omega, Jesus Christ

Fallen Leaves-Abandoned Branches

BY DAVID P. CARLSON

As this oak tree's limbs bend and sway in a late winter's blustery gust of recollected memories (all born of yesterday's summer meditations) she sheds her leaves like snow (or maybe like a serpent's skin upon the road of multi-misconceptions) but leaves a few for early spring to cover those untraveled lanes within her mind, ever on the path to her hometown back-yard patio, all sent tumbling silently down, thrumming along, all agape, recalling to their dismay those recanted hollow promises of joyous springtime escapades, all so imprudently scampering stealthily out of view from there atop of this great oak's perch of an imperious, impiously imbibed eidetically attained attitude, but still she sees and is content to watch her leaves be trod afoot there beneath those dead and dying wooden mazes, there to flip and sail through twigs and stems of abandoned nests of doves, sparrows, bluebirds, and tiny wrens and hummingbirds, finally down, pell-mellently resting on the forest's floor below, all of this left to steer another metaphor to parallel its self aversely into our lives upon the tangled branches of our lively forest's cultures. How green and tender is the new-born leaf upon the stem? How many years from spring to spring will come to pass before the savage task of growing faithful to the command of a fresh commitment to dedication. How many storms with lightening strikes can be endured before the return of early spring to count the ones upon the soiled and tattered truff of anonymity, then to hear the switch of man-made brooms to sweep away those countless disconcerted lives into assorted piles of resentful forms of repetitiousness—now from high above those tangled branches (of what she so often termed her brambles) she sees the hordes of stranded lives taken down by those winter winds of youthful pride, all laid to

rest in the notes of a mournful song on those solemn summer
night of deep regrets among those pellucidict forest noises,
Now to be whished away before the rise of the morning's light—such
is the mood of another era before her season ending storm of sorrow.
So resigned is her will (to cease to ere behold again the sight of another
begotten leaf at play upon a new mowed lawn of green, with her sister
oaks looming high above to provide the shade for another springtime
hope of another sunny day) – she lifts her limbs up high as if to pray
for one last test, for one more day; with a humble sway she bows her
head to receive her due, a rogue wind from an unseasonable front,
laced with a host of whirling gusts for her final fate of one horrendous
tornatic punch. This old oak was once like you and me, content to
abort her leaves before the rain, before the name of the Lord became
the only way to confront the loss of those perilous trials we've endured
in life, so designed to divert our ways. But now we see and recognize
that all that's left of the serpent's skin are flakes of forgiven sin to be
whisked away by the wind of another early spring. Days like leaves
will come and go, but the Lord we know as our Oak of life, whose
roots are deep within the sod will forever draw His strength to
renew his natural and grafted branches with all their multitudes of
new-born leaves of green, never to be let go, never to be forsaken.